Grasses and Peren

Introduction

This is a book outlining the principles for successfully planting shared spaces - the places we see and work at every day. The aim is to contribute to the discussion about how planted spaces can positively influence our surroundings, while being environmentally friendly, sustainable and stimulating. I am offering practical solutions, to overcome the challenges we face planting and maintaining functional spaces, in a changing climate. I hope you will be inspired to garden creatively, and motivated to care about the shared spaces surrounding us. After fifteen years gardening, I have written the book I wish I had read at the beginning of my gardening career.

Shared Space

Flower shows and historic gardens may be inspirational, or a reminder of former glory, and are frequently celebrated as examples of horticultural excellence. But preserved grand gardens often perpetuate an historic style of planting - with little relevance to modern horticultural practices in a changing climate. Contemporary show gardens look like unachievable aspirations, especially when made with virtually limitless budgets, and are difficult to visualise in another setting. A few skilfully designed plantings based on grasses and perennials (described as naturalistic) point the way forward, but these are outstanding examples of meticulous planting - with limited influence on garden designers and landscapers. Meanwhile, our towns and cities are made up of thousands of individuals, many of whom will never pay to visit a garden, and perhaps have no garden to call their own.

The reality of everyday life is somewhat different to the designed spaces of historic buildings, legacy plantings around sporting venues, and private (usually well-funded) pay-to-view gardens. It's the view that greets the vast majority of us every day that is important, made up of the spaces that surround us, shaping our immediate environment. The trip to the local supermarket, the school run, or walk into town, are the repeated journeys that reinforce our impressions of our immediate surroundings, good or bad. And when we arrive at our destination, the view from the office desk or glimpse of green space while walking between buildings, defines our own personal environment.

It is generally these views that I class as shared space, identified as an area which the general public see, have access to, or work at, on a daily basis. The scope is therefore wide ranging, and includes the gardens of private businesses such as offices, hotels and retail outlets, as well as public facilities - schools, surgeries and hospitals. I also include areas that are in public ownership via local authorities - parks, playgrounds and town centres. But why are the majority of our shared spaces so uninspiring, lacking vitality and dynamism, without any hint of design?

The planting in most shared spaces (with a few notable exceptions), appears repetitive, lacking imagination and purpose, and is therefore extremely forgettable. While we are all aware of the changing seasons, much of our shared space planting remains either relatively static (trees and evergreen shrubs), or is artificially altered - the change between summer and winter plant displays. Seasonality is usually achieved by temporary arrangements of densely packed bedding plants - a traditional, ingrained response to a perceived public demand.

Where local authorities are responsible for planting, the bedding displays presumably soak up the majority of the permitted budget; but how many hardy perennials, bulbs and grasses could have been purchased, planted and maintained over the years for the same cost? The overall effect could be built up year on year, and as any gardener knows, just a few seasons to allow for maturity will make a noticeable difference. So why do we allow our local authorities to effectively do just the opposite, and labour away at high maintenance bedding displays? Why not start to see our shared spaces as a giant garden, to appreciate and mature over a period of time, and train horticulturalists accordingly?

In business ownership the scenery is usually much more static, with minimal alteration following initial planting. Typically, a sea of evergreen shrubs dominates, clipped randomly into rounded shapes of varying size. The need to fill an empty space as quickly and painlessly as possible, usually results in plant groupings that are essentially unsustainable - too densely packed for growth rate, or too thinly spaced to prevent weed growth, and incompatible plant combinations. Unless an industry standard is adopted, or training improves, this type of result will continue to be the outcome for our shared spaces. And planting remains in place for years - so a few days' work (good or bad), becomes a legacy. The initial planting also has a significant impact on sustainability - how many planned maintenance visits be required annually, and how easy will pruning and weeding be? Unless the garden's maintenance is planned at conception, the likelihood of continued success diminishes with time.

A subtly changing scene, moving with the seasons can undoubtedly be achieved with carefully selected plants. We need to overcome our fear of disorder, and learn to maintain a diverse, yet harmonious combination of plants - an evolving ecological planting can still look neat and cared for. If hardy perennials are mixed with ornamental grasses and bulbs, the overall effect is one of diversity and movement, and continual variation. It should be noted that grasses are mainly perennials, but the sub-group of ornamental grasses is a distinct group in itself, and is therefore referred to as such.

It could be argued that the initial cost of a planting based predominantly on hardy perennials and grasses, is greater than that of a mass planting of evergreen shrubs. However, the shrubs take longer to mature, and may therefore require denser planting initially, followed by natural thinning in subsequent years, which is wasteful. Alternatively, supplementary underplanting may be required, that will eventually be in dry shade and struggle to survive. But the requirement for instant plant cover is seemingly irresistible, and the extra time spent planning and sourcing a diverse, stimulating plant selection, is seen as unwelcome delay and expenditure.

This is why our shared spaces often end up mass planted with tightly packed evergreens - quick, simple and seemingly cost effective. However, in my experience the mass planting leads almost immediately to natural thinning, as weaker plants die due to competition for light, water and nutrients. A secondary problem of embedded weeds then arises, and presents an ongoing maintenance problem. Eventually, the evergreens grow together and the obligatory pruning into a square or multiple rounded shapes inevitably follows, complete with self-sown shrubs/trees - never removed due to lack of knowledge or time constraints. The typical contractor's hedge cutter pruning regime frequently results in unsightly random cuts, leading to dieback and bare stems, contributing to an already unappealing view.

In the medium to long term, the hardy perennials/grasses planting (maybe with a few shrubs) wins, in aesthetics, low-maintenance requirements and longevity. Grasses and perennials are more forgiving of close planting, becoming self-sustaining, and potentially producing a surplus by splitting mature plants in spring and autumn, to create divisions. These can be planted in other parts of the garden, or swapped with other similar gardens, increasing biodiversity and plant stock.

To explore the difference that a more imaginative planting mix can make, I have selected as examples the Chesterton House Financial Planning Ltd walled garden, and the Woolley, Beardsleys & Bosworth LLP entrance garden - both part of The Chesterton House Group, Loughborough.

These are two of several gardens that I maintain, and illustrate how our shared spaces can be dramatically altered and improved, by plantings based on grasses and perennials. All the photographs in this chapter were taken in these gardens during summer 2019.

Chesterton House garden was created in the summer/autumn of 2017, from a neglected and overgrown space behind the offices. The walled garden held promise - a sheltered location in the historic conservation area of Loughborough. A landscaping company (Hortus Landscape Design and Construction) was employed to clear the ground, create raised beds and a seating area linked by paths, and lay the lawn. After that, the garden became my responsibility; a blank canvas, apart from a two small trees (fig and pear) which were already established and retained as specimens.

Woolley, Beardsleys & Bosworth (WBB) was quite the opposite, an existing garden, but in need of regenerating and updating. A few of the plants at WBB are not my introductions - *Phormium, Yucca, Euphorbia* and some *Hemerocallis* - but were retained as established plants that fulfilled a specific role, without detracting from the overall design. All existing shrubs (except subshrub *Vinca minor*) and climbers at WBB were gradually removed, from my arrival in April 2015, to 2018 when the garden was substantially replanted. Both gardens now share similar styles, with an attractive mix of planting designed to hold a person's interest, if only for a few seconds. This is essentially the difference between the forgettable, and the noteworthy. The plant mixtures are based around grasses and perennials; naturalistic patterns of repeated, but interchangeable combinations that are tried and tested.

The grasses form focal points and anchor the plantings - without them the gardens would appear static, lacking height and movement. As the grasses increase and flower, the foliage provides summer shade for nearby perennials. I use *Calamagrostis xacutiflora* 'Karl Foerster' and 'Overdam' for vertical height; both withstand rain quite well when in flower, despite temporarily bending almost to the ground, under the weight of accumulated moisture. *Panicum virgatum* 'Squaw' requires a moisture retentive soil, but is drought tolerant when established - occasional watering is necessary during dry summers.

Nassella tenuissima is indispensable, filling smaller gaps and reflecting sunlight from delicate inflorescences, while *Hakonechloa macra* spills over the sleeper edged beds in part shade. The *Carex* genus is wide and varied; I have chosen just three sedges - *Carex morrowii* 'Ice Dance' for dry shade, *Carex muskingumensis* and *Carex oshimensis* 'Everlime', for part shade on soils that don't dry out completely.

Two other grasses are used in my designs, *Miscanthus* and *Sesleria,* and have very different uses. *Miscanthus sinensis* 'Red Cloud' and 'Ferner Osten' can grow up to 1.5 metres tall, and are a substitute for shrubs. *Sesleria autumnalis* is a relatively low growing grass with the ability to blend in with perennials, and also looks good in containers. *Sesleria nitida* is a blue/grey version, and *Sesleria caerulea* provides blue foliage groundcover. Each grass is chosen for a specific use, and many others have been rejected over the years for lack of longevity, invasive seeding, lax habit in rich soils and poor stem retention during winter.

Now on to the perennials, the basis of flower colour and groundcover; these are chosen to give as long a flowering display as possible - as one plant finishes flowering, another nearby begins. I use several of the *Geranium* genus for reliable long flowering, attractive seed heads, and useful evergreen foliage - *Geranium macrorrhizum* 'Spessart' and 'Ingwersen's Variety', also *Geranium xcantabrigiense* 'Cambridge'. *Geranium nodosum* 'Hexham Big Eye' and *Geranium* 'Gerwat' (Rozanne) are both herbaceous, but have an exceptionally long flowering period, as does *Erigeron karvinskianus* 'Stallone'.

The *Persicaria* genus is wide and varied; I have selected the ones that seem to work reliably well. *Persicaria affinis* and the cultivar 'Darjeeling Red' are surprisingly drought tolerant when established, easy to divide, and good for filling gaps around grasses and under larger plants. *Persicaria amplexicaulis* 'Firetail', 'Golden Arrow' and 'Inverleith' take the place of small/medium sized shrubs, with the advantages of long flowering plants that are quick to bulk up. However, 'Inverleith' may require occasional watering during a very dry summer.

My plant choice has been whittled down over the years based on practicality, and availability. There is little point choosing plants that cannot be easily replaced if damaged, or die during the establishment phase - which can happen occasionally, even with the best care. All the gardens I look after share largely the same plant selection, so plants can be transferred, or increased by division - it's far easier to work with familiar plants and understand their limitations and strengths.

The beauty of choosing perennials is that many can be easily divided, and are more tolerant of damage in commercial settings than shrubs. That said, I do use a few plants categorised as shrubs/subshrubs; *Lavandula angustifolia* 'Hidcote' (easily replaced) and *Vinca minor* (easily propagated). At Chesterton there are a few *Cornus alba* 'Elegantissima', and a single *Cornus sericea* 'Cardinal' which are manipulated by late winter pruning to restrict size, and encourage brightly coloured fresh stems each year. WBB has a single *Rosa sp.*, which is a dwarf specimen. I rarely use roses now as they are prone to black spot (a fungal disease), but occasionally plant a floribunda; once the flowers are finished the entire flowering stem can be cut back, rather than removing individual spent flowers.

Quite a few *Hemerocallis* are dotted throughout the gardens, including 'Frans Hals', 'Stafford', 'Stella de Oro', 'Catherine Woodbery' and 'Pardon Me'. These robust and versatile plants are invaluable as their showy flowers light up the borders from early summer onwards, and appear tolerant of both sun and part shade, and quite dry soil. *Osteospermum jucundum* is a durable sun-loving groundcover, but does benefit from occasional applications of organic slug/snail pellets when required; snails hide under the evergreen foliage, and dying stems are an indication of pest damage. *Betonica officinalis* 'Hummelo' is useful anywhere in a planting, at the front with its flowers pushing up into overhanging grasses, or in between *Hemerocallis* and other taller perennials to cover bare soil. *Crocosmia xcrocosmiiflora* prefers moist soil, and is best planted a little more deeply than usual to prevent drying out during hot summers; it may be considered invasive, but holds vibrant contrasting flowers - I use it sparingly.

To conclude the perennials, I use *Sedum hybridum* as a low groundcover to fill gaps at the base of upright perennials, such as *Hylotelephium* 'Mr Goodbud' and *Hylotelephium* 'Herbstfreude', both previously categorised as *Sedum.* The *Hylotelephium* are easily divided and long lived, loved by bees and vine weevil alike! The latter are controlled by annual applications of nematodes, which I apply as a precaution even if there is no direct evidence of infestation.

Heuchera 'Blackberry Jam' is also susceptible to vine weevil, but I use it occasionally as a complete contrast to other perennials; having tried many *Heuchera* this one has proved the most reliable. A few *Heuchera* 'Obsidian' have been planted as a trial - the only way to thoroughly evaluate a cultivar is over time. *Veronica umbrosa* 'Georgia Blue' is an evergreen groundcover, and requires a moisture retentive soil or part shade. Its slender stems scramble through nearby *Cornus*, and root easily when in contact with the soil, making it useful for underplanting.

Although Chesterton House has a backdrop of red brick walls, I resisted the temptation to put in climbing roses; these would have limited the depth of planting available in the fairly narrow borders, and created a cottage garden impression - inappropriate for a corporate meeting space. Instead, I planted *Hydrangea anomala* subsp. *petiolaris*, two in the entrance courtyard (in dry shade), and two in the garden, linking the separate areas together. Chesterton House pergola has *Trachelospermum jasminoides* var. *pubescens* 'Japonicum' growing up and over it; I was concerned about winter hardiness, but so far they have survived a cold winter unscathed due to the sheltered location.

I also planted four *Phyllostachys nigra* (black bamboo, which are technically grasses), to screen neighbouring buildings with their evergreen, slightly arching upright culms. Finally, I have added bulbs (mainly *Narcissus* 'Tête à tête' and a few larger mixed cultivars) which increase each year, bringing a welcome burst of colour at a time when the grasses and herbaceous perennials are about to break from dormancy. I am not afraid to leave the gardens cut back to the ground and relatively bare for a brief period in late winter/early spring - the bulbs soon flower, and the annual cutting back is in itself an expression of seasonality. The expectation that a garden should perform evenly every month of the year is unrealistic, and undesirable. If dormancy is noticed, then so too is the subsequent new growth, which is welcomed.

Narcissus 'Tête à tête' is quite short, so the dying bulb leaves are quickly obscured by the grasses and herbaceous perennials fresh spring growth. I do use taller species of mixed *Narcissus* in shared spaces, (WBB has many which pre-date my arrival), but usually towards the back of borders, or among more vigorous perennials such as *Persicaria amplexicaulis*. It's important to leave the bulb leaves for 6-8 weeks after flowering, to build up next year's reserves before removing spent foliage. Placing the bulbs carefully among perennials minimises the visual distraction of the fading leaves.

Winter interest is held for as long as possible by allowing the grasses and herbaceous perennials to slowly fade away, and serves practical purposes for wildlife shelter and protection of the plant crown. This ecological approach to gardening is not new; in 1935 E.J.Salisbury wrote "...the unwisdom of cutting down the old stems of our herbaceous perennials too soon, unless our gardens be sheltered. The dead stems and leaves form a natural protection for the emerging shoots against the icy winds of winter." (The Living Garden). It's always a balancing act at this time of year; I tend to cut back perennials when the sharp winter frosts have reduced the foliage to a brown heap, and there is nothing more to be gained from retaining it. I leave the grasses for as long as possible; the skeleton of the garden is evocative - a reminder of a season almost spent, but the promise of another to follow.

The winter cutting back is therefore phased, and depends on the condition and growth habit of the individual plants. *Erigeron karvinskianus* forms a protective green mound until spring, whereas *Carex muskingumensis* starts regrowing as early as late December, and is best cut back then. Standing stems of *Calamagrostis*, *Hakonechloa*, *Panicum* and *Miscanthus* are selected points of interest, which can be left until late February or even early March; it all depends on spring's arrival, and how much form the grasses are holding. Cutting back needs to be done carefully to avoid damaging nearby emerging bulb leaves - late cutting of grasses can be done a little higher if necessary.

Cutting back on a large scale can be done just prior to the bulb leaves breaking through - and this could easily become standard practice for grounds maintenance in our shared spaces - quick, easy and effective. This type of maintenance regime is certainly more straightforward and cost effective than multiple visits to repeatedly trim the same shrubs/hedges, throughout the growing season. Where mass plantings of evergreens mature over time, the end result is often the equivalent of an informal hedge - repeated pruning at a convenient height for the contractor.

At some gardens I look after, I have cut shrubs and hedges as often as weekly or fortnightly during a warm, wet summer; this is not a viable solution for shared spaces, especially with limited budgets. But the grasses and perennials planting sails through the growing season with little or no cutting. Instead, the time is focused on more productive interventions - perhaps a few weeds pulled, or some divisions, watching for pests and diseases and subtle alterations to the design.

Admittedly, more horticultural knowledge is required to maintain plantings based on hardy perennials and grasses; knowing when to divide perennials, keeping a stock of suitable replacements for short lived plants, such as *Nassella tenuissima*, and awareness of which grasses require annual cutting back. This could easily be resolved by better training for our horticulturalists, offset by the efficiencies of self-sustaining plantings.

My top tips for creating an interesting and diverse shared space are as follows; select a small number of reliably performing plants and repeat them at intervals throughout the grounds - this gives consistency and cohesion, especially in a corporate setting. Aim for an achievable maintenance regime which is not fussy - no staking, minimal deadheading, and targeted supplementary watering only in the driest of summers.

Once I have started work on a shared space project, the garden quickly becomes a shared enthusiasm. Staff and management team see the future potential from the already apparent improvement, and this usually results in more time and money being found - greater commitment is made as the benefits become obvious. As members of the public visit the site, improvements are noticed, and commented on. I have been asked for divisions of admired plants, and questions about the plant selection; so interest in horticulture is encouraged, and plant diversity grows. If a shared space is neglected, none of this happens.

What is it that makes a shared space worthwhile? Is it seasonal changes making a difference to the daily routine - or regular glimpses of the natural world? Is it simply a new perspective, like a walk in the park away from the office desk? Our daily views are part of us, shaping our impressions of the world around us and directly affecting our quality of life. Perhaps this explains why we put so much time and effort into our own gardens - it's also the view we see every day.

Planted Space

We live in a country with constantly changing, unpredictable weather patterns. Over the last few years, England has experienced intense and sustained periods of drought, high rainfall leading to flooding, and some very cold winters. Temporary climatic fluctuations can seem endless, as the weather conditions continue largely unaltered for several months. Successful plantings should be able to cope with short term climatic volatility, and become self-sustaining. A thriving planted space is a colony of aesthetically pleasing, compatible plants, with the inherent capability to evolve and mature. Gently managing the ebb and flow of plants intermingling, while preserving the original design objective, is the art of gardening. The long term stability of a planting is dependent on its ability to acclimatise, or decisively withstand varying climatic conditions.

Charles Darwin's sometimes misunderstood work is often referred to as *survival of the fittest*. Although fitness is undoubtedly an aid to survival, the ability of well adapted species to survive and reproduce was the tenet of Darwin's theory. Plant communities we perceive as inherently stable, such as wildflower meadows and grassland, are in fact very active and mobile when devoid of human intervention. The natural plant community is constantly in a state of flux - maybe even eventually giving way to shrubs or forest and ceasing to exist in its earlier form. In nature, every available niche is filled by a plant able to exploit the given conditions, so the plant is always matched perfectly to its environment. As environmental conditions alter, so too does the composition of the plant community - either progressively with permanent alteration, or in cycles of regeneration following short term disturbance, usually caused by wildfires.

To garden successfully, it's important to draw a distinction between the practically possible with minimal difficulty, and attempting the virtually impossible by constant interventions. With experimentation and experience, an interesting planting mix that is diverse, as well as durable, may be designed. This is achieved by an understanding of plant tolerance, growth rate, and local knowledge of the soil and climate.

Attempting to establish a plant, in a very different environment to its natural habitat, leads to inevitable struggle and disappointment. If natural habitat conditions are disregarded, regular interventions are necessary to compensate, and tip the environmental factors back in favour of survival. Common expressions of these interventions are temporary protection (fleece, glasshouse), regular watering (distinct from initial establishment phase watering), nutrient supplementation and repeated applications of pest/disease control products.

Today, gardening is all about sustainability with minimal intervention; not only is this approach easier, it is also mindful of resource use. The likelihood of a plant successfully establishing and thriving is determined by the gardener, when selecting the final planting position; frequently described as *right plant, right place*. However, we need to move towards a greater understanding, not just of the individual plant and its intended location, but rather how the whole garden responds as a collective, a <u>community</u>. How a planting matures and interacts determines not just its aesthetic appeal, but also its lifespan - which is directly related to the suitability of the plants selected.

Our existing parameters for suitability are usually restricted to soil type and hardiness, as well as sun/shade tolerance and moisture requirements. A plant's ability to withstand extreme weather is commonly expressed only as a hardiness rating, and a location within a hardiness temperature zone. But these are limited standards - unable to take into account temporary, but prolonged climatic fluctuations. A plant may well survive at -5°C, but might not cope with two months of waterlogged soil.

We fail to consider root restriction (minimal competition for root development when planting); vigour in our soil as opposed to natural habitat (excessive nutrient availability); and lax habit caused by excess moisture/lack of predictable summer heat. These oversights give rise to interventions, such as regular watering, staking, and limiting the spread of prolific self-seeding and strongly rhizomatous/stoloniferous plants. These interventions, (which some would call gardening) are necessary to achieve a desirable result; but would be unnecessary or at least limited with a selection of self-sustaining plants.

By randomly assembling disparate genera and species together, we are attempting to circumvent countless millennia of unstoppable evolutionary activity. The natural tendency thereafter will be for competition over resources - light, nutrients and moisture - and over time, the inevitable result will be survival (not necessarily of the fittest), but of the most suited to the prevailing conditions. This is especially true of plantings in shared spaces, where plant-specific interventions may be limited due to time constraints. Eventually, only the most compatible plants will emerge triumphant, coexisting within an ecosystem; or alternatively one plant will gradually dominate at the expense of all others - monoculture by default. Although large scale monocultures may have their place - as part of an overall design - most of England's shared spaces are too small for this to be successful. We need variety, and interest for as much of the year as possible.

In our shared spaces, we often experience the worst of both worlds; overcrowded plantings filled with two or three varieties of evergreen shrubs, neither monoculture nor truly mixed planting.

Either imaginative design was absent at conception, or inappropriate maintenance over time has led to plant losses and gradual consolidation. Poorly maintained but initially innovative plantings, such as rain gardens, wildflower meadows, and wildlife areas often appear unkempt and unloved, and lack forward planning to achieve the design objectives. I have observed the planting at high profile city centre regeneration projects (obviously at great expense), where shade dependent plants are in full sun, large specimen grasses grouped too close together for their eventual size, and plants requiring sun placed in shade - or shade to be as nearby plants expand. These errors demonstrate a lack of basic horticultural knowledge, and represent a missed opportunity. There is little point investing in high quality hard landscaping - often at public expense - only to plant poorly, leading to inevitable disappointment.

Where planting design is evident, the designer's underlying intentions and aspirations often become confused and unfulfilled. This may be due to a lack of specific instructions to contractors, or incorrect interpretation and execution of planting plans by landscapers. Failure to anticipate the growth rate of plants, and understand their requirements for successful establishment, inevitably leads to incomplete plantings - never attaining full potential. Too often, the three key elements for a successful planting - design, planting and maintenance - are separated by incompatible goals, overambitious projects, insufficient funding and a lack of skilled horticulturalists.

There is an undoubted skill to designing, planting and maintaining a sustainable, manageable planting - which will endure, albeit with subtle alterations. The basis for successful garden design and management should be a selection of compatible, versatile plants; grasses and evergreen/herbaceous perennials are ideal for fulfilling this role. As perennials spread the spaces between plants is eliminated and a gentle intermingling takes place - a meeting of ecological harmony rather than a fight for survival. This is illustrated by the photographs in this chapter, taken at Orchard Surgery, Kegworth and Chesterton House Financial Planning Ltd, Loughborough.

Over time, plants spreading by rhizomes and stolons might need a little separating from nearby plants, to maintain the design objectives - appropriate plant selection, according to microclimate should limit aggressive spreading tendencies. Some deciduous grasses require division to maintain vigour every four years or so, and any groundcover growing through the crown can be removed at the same time. The beneficial process of regeneration and separation leads to the production of small plants (divisions), and these can be used to cover any remaining bare soil, or fill gaps left by failures.

In the first year or two of a new planting project, I divide to conquer; bare soil is the enemy, and one of the easiest (and cheapest) ways to cover it is by dividing perennials, in spring or autumn. Growing from seed is an option, but the divisions are instant semi-mature plants and soon bulk up. A living mulch of plants quickly fills in gaps, and creates unity and flow throughout the garden, by repeating the same plant in similar locations. Groundcover beneficially suppresses weeds, prevents erosion, keeps the soil cool in summer, and if evergreen takes up moisture in winter - preventing waterlogging around the roots of dormant perennials. Apart from these attractions, why have bare soil when you can grow a plant? Unoccupied space is rare in nature - if a space can be colonised by a plant, it probably will be. I allow creeping colonisation to enhance the planting, moving it towards a softer, more natural appearance.

The design at the outset will necessarily alter over time, depending on the development speed of each large specimen or plant grouping - but the original objective can remain constant. If one particular plant starts to spread and become just a little too prevalent, I dig out a few pieces and distribute these elsewhere in the garden, or freely across other sites I maintain - this increases plant diversity across several gardens. Otherwise, provided the overall appearance is acceptable, I am happy to allow spreading as the plants determine. There will always be an element of natural unpredictability, no matter how carefully the design is balanced to the site. A year of high rainfall may slightly favour one genus or species over another, and a long hot summer or exceptionally cold winter will have a similar affect.

When planting, I often draw a circle in the soil around the plant (while still in its pot, in the intended planting position), using a spade edge or stick to indicate the diameter of intended growth. This is not necessarily the same thing as <u>fully</u> grown; rather the intention to fill an allotted space with a chosen plant. When allocating a space, I am planning plant size based on the premise that the plant can be successfully pruned, or gently restricted by coexisting with nearby plants. By drawing circles, I allow room for several grasses and perennials to fill a space, without either becoming too crowded or appearing too sparse. The result should be a largely predictable, reliable planting, with significant colour and interest for most of the year.

I aim to cover almost all bare soil with plants, within two years of the initial planting and as much as possible within one year. This covering is not apparent all year, but during the growing season it's important to have the minimum of bare soil to prevent weed germination, and for aesthetics. As herbaceous perennials lose their foliage and seasonal interest, and gaps appear in late autumn and early winter, underplanted bulbs are added.

I rarely use shrubs, other than *Cornus* or *Cotinus*, both of which may be pruned hard annually, but still have a natural appearance afterwards. For instance, when using *Cornus* I will underplant with groundcover and/or spring bulbs, and coppice the *Cornus* annually, thus keeping its size in relation to surrounding plants.

There is little point endlessly clipping a shrub into a rounded shape or square, simply because it has been planted in a space unable to accommodate its natural, free branching size. The only point in maintaining a clipped shrub is to make a hedge, or intended topiary within the design. Gradually, I am removing constrained and clipped shrubs and replanting where possible with *Miscanthus*, which can be left indefinitely without division. The *Miscanthus* increase steadily and predictably in size, and require just one annual cut back - far easier!

I apply the same low-maintenance principle to climbers, choosing a few that are tractable, rather than those producing copious quantities of vegetative growth, which must be controlled. I see little value in struggling to maintain high-maintenance climbers, which flower for a reliably short interval, before effectively becoming a passenger in the garden for the remainder of the year.

After fifteen years professional gardening, I have settled on using a limited selection of tried-and-tested plants. The list is not exhaustive; rather an ongoing exchange, as plants are added and others are rejected. For instance, *Tiarella cordifolia* provides useful groundcover fulfilling several roles - colourful evergreen foliage which varies through the seasons, flowers in spring, and spreading habit. But vine weevil can decimate *Tiarella*, and twice yearly applications of nematodes (*Steinernema kraussei*) are required to give some measure of control. The expense is hard to justify for commercial clients on a large scale - and is it really sustainable?

I am using *Persicaria affinis* as a replacement, a versatile groundcover, with flower and foliage interest. The *Persicaria* appears more drought tolerant, with an attractive quality of producing redder foliage under stress. In temporarily dry shade, it sits waiting patiently for rain, while nearby *Tiarella* wilts. There is always a temptation to intervene early at the first sign of drought stress in a planting - but by doing so, I learn nothing. How much stress can a particular plant take, and will it fully recover following a period of sustained water deprivation? By utilising the same plants, in different locations and microclimates, I gain a working knowledge of plants' growth rates and attributes. It's better to know a few plants intimately, and place them accurately, than have a superficial knowledge over a wide spectrum.

When a planting is designed, there may be a temptation to maintain a fully planted garden indefinitely, by pruning and weeding, watering at the first sign of stress, but rarely accepting change. By strictly maintaining a plant in a chosen location, year in, year out, regardless of altered circumstances or suitability, we are gardening against nature's intentions. Natural selection has determined beneficial traits, survival mechanisms and habitat range, of each and every plant we decide to use. We can utilise these attributes when planting, by matching the planting position as closely as possible with the plant's natural habitat. If this approach is followed for each plant, a sustainable community may be successfully constructed - a planting with an ecosystem unique to the locality, interconnected with the microclimate.

In abandoned or lightly gardened spaces, a constant ebb and flow of colonisation (by plants spreading or seeding) is evident, according to localised conditions such as availability of light, nutrients and moisture. These essential ingredients for survival vary over time, influenced by nearby plants maturing (expanding tree canopy, large grasses increasing), and temporary extremes, such as waterlogging, cold/frost and drought - potentially causing casualties. Any space will be quickly filled with quiet efficiency, by a plant suited to the conditions.

To the gardener, altered circumstances should represent fresh design and planting opportunities, by selecting appropriate plants to succeed where others have failed. Spaces vacated by failures can be filled with self-sown offspring from nearby thriving plants, or divisions. Different sizes of plants in varying stages of maturity help give a more natural feel to a successful planting. I have a problem with flower show demonstration gardens, with perfect plants all the same relative size, all flowering at the same time - it looks contrived. Natural, self-sustaining plantings will always have variety and variation, seasonal flowering, self-seedlings, and senescence. Why not demonstrate and celebrate reality, rather than unachievable aspirations?

Designing a compatible plant community may initially appear daunting, but the fundamental requirement is to picture fully grown plants in the mind. I resist the temptation to pack in as many different plants as possible (the curse of the domestic garden), and instead try to repeat combinations that work. This gives a sense of unity and stability to plantings, with harmony created by using different cultivars of the same species, and different species of the same genus. The similarities of plant character provide consistency and cohesion.

Plants have three dimensions - vertical stems and foliage/flower height, horizontal stems and foliage spread (including rhizomes and stolons), and roots. These dimensions comprise a growth strategy, and each individual plant must have sufficient room to establish, develop, and mature sufficiently to fulfil its role, without unintended restriction. This means not introducing undue competition from nearby plants during the design and planting process. For instance, a group of relatively deep rooted grasses such as *Calamagrostis* x*acutiflora* 'Overdam', could be underplanted with a spreading groundcover of *Persicaria affinis* and *Erigeron karvinskianus* 'Stallone'. For this to be successful, the plants should ideally be planted at the same time, and develop together.

The *Persicaria* and *Erigeron* will supress weeds, and act as living mulch - the groundcover mainly occupy a different space to the grasses, both above and below ground. There is minimal competition where the roots meet in the topsoil; the grasses have the advantage of a deeper root network, to compensate for the moisture extracted by the surrounding groundcover. Where the foliage meets above ground there is a gentle intermingling, with minimal competition for resources.

Alternatively, colonisation may be *deliberately* restricted by similar plants competing for identical resources, within the same space, both above and below ground level. Groundcover plants will meet and intermingle at the meeting point, but unless one has a far stronger growth rate than the others, the planting will remain balanced and stable. Colonisation is effectively checked by selecting plants with identical requirements, and becomes coexistence. A limited, thoughtfully researched plant selection can create planted space that is self-reliant, resilient, easily repeatable, and requires <u>less</u> maintenance over time.

The reason why so many car park plantings are filled with overcrowded, ubiquitous shrubs is because of the perceived reliability of evergreen plants. To make matters worse, any seasonal flowering of evergreens is usually obliterated by repeated cutting. The irrepressible desire to plant an instant garden, without worrying about dormancy and seasonality, has become the landscaper's default position.

We need to introduce a compilation of plants - a recipe for success - based around grasses and perennials to create imaginative, long lasting plantings that work in a variety of situations. To that end, I would like to see plant encyclopaedias and on-line resources describe the plants' natural habitat, and expand on the conditions there. If the intended planting position/microclimate can be matched reasonably closely with the plants' natural habitat, the chances of success are greatly increased.

At present, there is a knowledge gap to be filled as far as perennials are concerned, which can only be resolved by trial and error, leading to empirical evidence. By observing and understanding plants' responses to specific environments and climatic volatility, we are gradually learning how to build sustainable plant communities. As our knowledge expands, our planting decisions can become sound, researched and innovative, rather than based simply on hope or intuition. Inspirational shared spaces that are creatively planted and well maintained, can serve as a template to be adopted and modified.

A well designed planted space should have the inherent ability to withstand extreme and varying climatic conditions, and become self-sustaining; the fewer interventions a garden has from the gardener, the more successful it really is. We need to learn to accept a flexible concept for gardening, based on ecologically sound decisions; employing minimal, thoughtful, short term interventions, to establish successful plantings and manage change. The balance can be tipped in favour of thriving plantings, if we are prepared to engage with nature's pointers and make the necessary adjustments. The gardener's axiom *right plant, right place* has evolved into review, revise, and replant.

Functional Space

Planting our visible environment fulfils a basic human need, to connect with nature and the wider landscape. We feel inexorably drawn to landscapes we perceive as natural or seemingly untouched by mankind; although in reality most are the result of previous agricultural activity. Our appreciation of nature rises while walking in woodland or looking at open grassland, moorland or wildflower meadow - definitive and recognisable landscapes, distinct from arbitrary urban planting. If the appreciated landscape can somehow be imported into the largely sterile urban environment, we can all benefit from a collective feeling of well-being.

Plantings that contain elements drawn from familiar natural landscapes are more likely to be accepted, appreciated and cared for; becoming successful and sustainable, by inspiring a collective desire to conserve and maintain something considered worthwhile. Our urban planted spaces provide much needed stability and continuity - anchor points in a fast changing world. This does not mean that plantings should be static; the continual maintenance and evolution of our shared spaces is always watched, and well regarded by passers-by. People feel comfortable and safer in an area that is obviously well maintained, and enjoy seeing gardening in progress.

We also notice, however, when our shared spaces are unkempt, poorly maintained, or carelessly planted; in which case positive feelings give way to negative emotions. Local authority cuts to landscape design and maintenance budgets can lead to wider reaching decline, making housing and local amenities less desirable. This in turn creates despair and a feeling of helplessness as a response to the neglect, and causes significant harm to community cohesion and well-being. Our shared spaces should be at the forefront of a focus on crime prevention, climate change mitigation and public health initiatives; transforming bland, unimaginative plantings into uplifting and purposeful spaces for the community.

The way in which a shared space is designed relates directly to its function (whether intentional or not), and its lifespan.
An overgrown planting conceals litter, creates a claustrophobic feeling, and appears dark and threatening at dusk. A well designed planting arranges growth at an appropriate height, keeps walkways visible and inviting, and filters reassuring light through the plants.

The photographs in this chapter were taken at Danaher & Walsh Group Ltd, Mountsorrel and Orchard Surgery, Kegworth and show the borders surrounding car parking areas. The first impression visitors have on arrival is of grounds that are well designed, neat and cared for - and staff working there every day appreciate the garden views, watching and welcoming seasonal changes.

The pictures illustrate how a car park can serve multiple functions; a thoroughfare, a place to park, an interesting viewpoint with pollinator friendly plants - softening the signage and hard landscaping. Note the use of *Calamagrostis xacutiflora*, with strong upright habit, mixed with *Miscanthus sinensis*, surrounded by flowering perennials. I aim to provide flowers for as long as possible throughout the year - these are always appreciated and commented on. Provided the design has colour and interest, it will hold a person's gaze if only for a moment, and lift their spirits.

It's essential to ensure quality, interest and longevity in the plantings that clean our air, and soften the urban landscape. We urgently need to repair the ecological damage caused by urban development, and exponential population growth. This is only achievable by incorporating planting into every urban expansion plan as a first response, not an afterthought - and integrating extensive planting into the existing built environment.

Grasses and perennials are an ideal answer to the challenge of sustainable plantings in urban areas, containing recognisable elements of grassland and wildflower meadows, without seeking to reproduce an archetype. I do not subscribe to the view that plantings must conform entirely to a recognised archetype (such as a meadow, grassland or woodland), in order to be interpreted, understood and accepted. Provided plants are well suited to the site, and can develop into a sustainable, compatible planting which appears to be gardened successfully, then the design will be accepted.

Natural landscapes can never be copied exactly; only adapted by designing plantings to promote positive responses from us, and ecosystem balance for wildlife. Our urban areas have already altered the landscape irrevocably, so attempting to somehow restore plantings to a natural state is untenable - the soil conditions and surrounding microclimates are far removed from that which previously existed. We need to design and maintain innovative plantings, guaranteed to work in the world we have now, based on science and practicality.

Rather than relying on plants considered native to the British Isles, I will use any plant with potential, from anywhere, provided it will establish within a community of compatible plants. There is currently a mistaken assumption that native plants (as opposed to non-native plants, often labelled as exotics), are ideally suited to geographic region of origin and pollinators, without question. In reality, native plants may succumb to freshly introduced pathogens and react poorly to a swiftly altering climate.

The use of the term *exotics* conjures up images of large leafy plants from the tropics, with huge flowers and invasive tendencies - which definitely don't belong locally. The use of the word exotic seems prejudicial, implying inferiority and even danger; which is why I prefer the term of *native*, and *non-native*.

The insistence by some designer's on using solely native plants, is effectively a determination that a given moment in time (usually in the past), is somehow ecologically superior - and overlooks the positive and scientific arguments for planting non-natives. There is little point constructing plantings based solely on region of origin, rather than usefulness and resilience. Plant communities alter all the time and nature is never static; and the definition of native plants is also somewhat subjective - we cannot know for certain how plants were moved and used by early humans. Can we safely assume that a plant is native to a given environment, simply because a plant hunter happened to discover it there - probably quite recently in terms of our evolution?

A further complication arises with the propagation and widespread distribution of cultivated varieties (cultivars), which may (occasionally) be naturally occurring and selected for cultivation, or produced by horticultural means. When cultivars arise from native plants they are sometimes accepted as natives, and called *nativars*. I rather think it is a little too late to hold a native vs. non-native discussion; by now any fertile imported non-native plants will have produced limitless amounts of seed, most of which will lay dormant in the soil, awaiting favourable conditions to germinate.

In my first attempts at garden design I planted *Deschampsia cespitosa* 'Goldtau' in a variety of situations. The results were disappointing; the grasses gradually declined during a succession of cold, wet winters, succumbing to crown rot and failing to regenerate with any vigour, following the annual cut back. Instead, I planted *Calamagrostis xacutiflora* 'Overdam' and 'Karl Foerster', both of which have performed reliably, without any losses whatsoever.

The origin of the hybrid *Calamagrostis xacutiflora* is Eurasian (where both its parents come from), so it should logically have a greater degree of hardiness than *Deschampsia cespitosa*, which originates from cool temperate parts of North America, Europe and eastern Asia. It is also worth mentioning the *Deschampsia* had a tendency to self-sow prolifically, making it less well suited to plantings in shared spaces, where budgets are tight and time for weeding limited. The *Calamagrostis* cultivars have never produced fertile seeds, making them immensely useful in shared spaces, with their strong vertical outlines.

The ability of plants (native or non-native) to self-sow can be a problem, especially if one plant is particularly fertile - thereby adulterating the design and potentially decreasing biodiversity. Using grasses and perennials that self-sow less, (or not at all) in our climate, preserves design objectives and limits maintenance weeding. *Miscanthus sinensis* is a perfect example of a versatile non-native plant; pest and disease resistant in England, non-invasive and no viable seed produced. The stems stand tall throughout winter holding feathery inflorescences, making a perfect habitat for insects.

I have chosen plants that self-sow beneficially, and assist with linking together a planting gradually, to give a variety of sizes of the same species. *Nassella tenuissima* is quite short lived, and gently self-sows to usefully reproduce itself; and in doing so moves the planting towards a more natural appearance. Unwanted seedlings are easily removed, and usually replanted elsewhere. The same applies to *Erigeron karvinskianus*, which spreads seed around itself filling gaps, to make a floriferous groundcover - I view it as productive rather than invasive.

Provided the plant will definitely not cause harm to the wider environment, why not use it, regardless of origin? If plants cannot adapt quickly enough to climate change, then human intervention through introducing alternatives is a force for good, ensuring pollinators are protected and soil health improved. A diversity of plants are beneficial for soil health, as different rooting depths prevent erosion and improve soil structure, allowing water, nutrients and air to circulate. As my experience with the *Deschampsia* shows, some plants are sensitive to extreme climatic conditions, and consequently perform poorly. To ensure resilience and longevity in urban plantings, any plant from a similar temperature zone to our own that can be successfully utilised, should be.

Designing a functional planting embraces not only visual impact, but also considers pollinators, insects and birds, and looks after the topsoil for the long term future. The challenge we face is to make our world a much better place, in spite of human predominance and industrialisation. This challenge has never been more important, because we understand that our existence is dependent on the health of the natural world.

Maintained Space

Plant choice determines garden maintenance requirements for years to come. The overused term *low-maintenance* is somewhat subjective, and fails to convey the essence of sustainable, compatible plant communities. At gardens I maintain, I prefer to look at the likelihood of future interventions, from establishment watering through to plant divisions on maturity, as the basis for planned maintenance. The planting should be suited to the site, with a plan to adequately maintain the garden (and improve if necessary), without exceeding the available budget. By establishing an anticipated ongoing cost, the long term future and design objectives are protected.

Each site is also included (with the owner's permission) in a plant swap and share scheme; enabling divisions and self-sown plants to be transferred, free of charge, between all the gardens taking part. This increases biodiversity, keeps costs down for everyone, and ensures a ready supply of replacement plants in case of failure. It's also an insurance against lack of retail availability - there is no point using plants that are both hard to source, and difficult to propagate. I use the selection of plants referred to in "Shared Space", at every garden I plant and maintain - not necessarily all of them and never in exactly the same arrangement - but each site has the same recognisable character. All the plants are either readily available at nearby nurseries, or are easy to divide - and some reproduce by self-sowing. The majority of the plant stock is sourced locally, with a few favourites brought in by mail order from other parts of the country.

I tend to specialise in renovating neglected gardens at shared spaces, and my initial response is always to remove unwanted plants and mulch heavily, if the site cannot be planted immediately. This serves several purposes; to create a blank canvas, ensure a good measure of weed control, and produce better topsoil as organic matter decomposes. The mulching also buys time especially on larger sites - as the garden is gradually developed and planted, everywhere looks well-kept.

I use woodchips as my initial mulch, sourced from local tree surgeons, laid down at approximately 80-100mm depth. This sounds a lot, but a wet winter soon breaks down the smaller pieces of wood, and any less allows weeds to push through. Some really tough weeds such as bramble and bindweed always emerge, and these are treated with a systemic herbicide. Once a site is under control and planted, the plants should ideally provide sufficient groundcover as living mulch.

Some grounds are just too expansive to plant up entirely, or have difficult areas in which to establish plants, such as under tree canopies, or where builder's rubble has been left just below the surface. These areas are mulched using woodchips every year or two, depending on the rate of decomposition. I remove the previous layer of decomposing mulch from around the base of trees first, to prevent a build up against the trunk. It's also a good idea to strip off a layer of previous mulch/topsoil against kerbs and path edges - this means the fresh woodchips can sit against the concrete edge, without spilling over onto the hard landscaping. Birds pick through the mulch as they search for food, and keeping the woodchips just below edges prevents too much being flicked out.

Plants can gradually be established where possible, but difficult areas do always take longer to cover. *Carex morrowii* 'Ice Dance' is always a good candidate for shade and poor soil; regular watering is required while the plants establish. This sedge is a rhizomatous spreader, and will tolerate mulching; as the woody material breaks down it replicates the sedge's native woodland environment. The photographs in this chapter illustrating mulching and other practical points were taken at Danaher & Walsh Group Ltd, Mountsorrel; Chesterton House Financial Planning Ltd, Loughborough and Orchard Surgery, Kegworth.

On freshly prepared landscaped sites where heavy mulching is not required, a light top up of organic compost (about 15mm) is useful during the winter for the first year or two after planting, especially on clay soil. The compost evens out any low spots, helps shield roots exposed by frost heave during the first winter, and flocculates clay. Shrubs and evergreen perennials should not have mulch heaped around them, as this may cause the stems to rot. Herbaceous perennials can be mulched, especially when dormant; new growth will push through a light layer of organic compost mulch in spring. A small amount of compost can be scattered around shrubs and under the outer leaves of perennials retaining winter foliage, so the planting appears neat and uniform.

I also use organic compost sourced from local recycling centres when planting, rather than peat based products. There is a suggestion that plants grown in peat prefer a peat mix around the rootball when planted, to encourage their roots to grow out into soil containing a familiar element. The reluctance of plants to put out fresh roots into soil is probably attributed to nursery plants being sold too late, when the roots have wound into a tight circle and the plant is described as *pot-bound*. If this is the case, I use secateurs and make three or four cuts into the base of the rootball; this encourages fresh new roots to emerge from the damaged areas, and into the soil.

Although it is true that a plant will have developed an association with the growing medium, and it is helpful to have a <u>similar</u> environment to continue steady growth, similar does not mean identical. The aids to growth are more likely to be a well-drained soil, with readily available moisture and nutrients, supported by regular supplementary watering as required - especially during the first year after planting. If the soil is particularly poor, and has too high a sand or clay content, I mix organic compost into the soil when planting, and spread a thin layer around the plant as mulch.

It would be easier, of course if the nursery trade produced plants in a growing medium closer to topsoil, rather than peat, which is unlikely to be found naturally in the vast majority of gardens. There are sound arguments for growing plants in organic compost; I have tried this myself, using the same product I supplement the planting out process with. Plants grow more slowly, as the compost is somewhat denser than peat, and the roots are therefore likely to be stronger, with inherent ability to establish soundly. The light and open peat based growing media used in the horticultural industry is consistent and adaptable, and produces fine roots very quickly, whereas organic products can vary in quality. But the price for speed and efficiency is using a finite resource, lacking commonality with the final planting location.

During the planting process, I place the plant in the ground - still in its container. This enables me to check if the plant looks right at soil level, and fits in with nearby plants in the intended planting position. It's easier to gauge the impact and suitability of the plant, and make a slight adjustment at this stage before finally planting.

If the plant has a lot of overhanging foliage, or has quite brittle shoots and leaves, I initially plant the container, not the plant. The soil (and organic compost if required) can be firmed around the container, up to the top - the container can then be removed, and the rootball inserted into the perfectly sized hole.

It's easy to gently push a bit more soil/compost around under the leaves as a final firming up, rather than having to fill the planting hole completely and risk damaging the foliage. Finally, I make sure the new plant is well watered in, and water regularly until established. With larger plants I pour water into the planting hole several times as the soil is firmed around the rootball, to reach the bottom of the roots and soak into the surrounding topsoil.

To reduce weed germination, it's important to minimise soil disturbance during planting; turning over excessive amounts of topsoil simply encourages dormant weed seeds to germinate. Sometimes weed problems only emerge after planting, as bramble and bindweed regenerate from deep down pieces of root - small pieces of root may be missed when digging out established weeds. The only practical way of dealing with this is to target the fresh young leaves with a systemic herbicide, and repeat as necessary.

One solution for targeted spraying in a planting is to use plastic tubes, made from old downpipes - the tubes are pressed into the soil over the emerging weeds - and the sprayer nozzle inserted into the top for a brief spray of herbicide. This is a better solution than using a spray shield attached to the sprayer, as the tubes remain in place while the herbicide dries.

The best time to do this is early/mid spring, before the target weeds have a chance to strengthen, and to minimise the risk of accidental contamination as nearby perennials extend their leaves. I see no problem whatsoever with using targeted herbicide and pesticide treatments; there is no point watching a plant die, or struggling with persistent weeds when a solution is readily available, and cultural controls have failed, or are impractical.

Research and technology have ensured that today's treatments are probably the safest ever, so it's ironic that so much fuss is made now about the appropriate use of chemicals. Without glyphosate and selective herbicides, it would be impossible to keep the shared spaces I maintain looking neat and cared for, by routinely controlling weed growth in car parks, paths and lawns. Acetic acid based formulations are excellent for moss and liverwort control on hard surfaces, but give poor control of established perennial weeds. Future technology may provide herbicide free weed control, but until promising innovations become mainstream and affordable, we can only use what is available and effective.

As evergreen perennials start to grow in spring, it's sometimes beneficial to cut back and encourage robust new growth, and remove trailing stems overhanging paths and raised beds. This allows light onto the current season's growth at the base of the plant, and may also assist with cultural pest control. *Osteospermum jucundum* shelters snails and caterpillars beneath its spreading foliage; if the plant is cut back almost to the ground in spring, the birds can pick these off, leading to fewer applications of organic slug/snail pellets later in the season. The cutting back will result in later flowering, but gives a fresh green look in the meantime as new growth begins, and the plant sits a little lower at the front of the border.

I try to minimise green waste produced by routine cutting during the growing season, by repeatedly trimming topiary features and small-leaved hedges on a weekly basis. The tiny amounts of clippings produced are easily absorbed under nearby plants and decompose, returning nutrients to the soil.

The practice of cutting little-and-often can also be applied to lawns, cutting twice a week using a mower fitted with mulching blades. Rather than take clippings away for recycling, the finely cut grass remains on the lawn, and quickly decomposes, returning nutrients to the soil - reducing the need for fertiliser treatments. I use a mower with a standard blade/grass box in autumn, to pick up fallen leaves and keep the lawns looking tidy.

Grass has an amazing ability to regenerate and tolerate repeated cutting, and a freshly mown lawn instantly makes a garden look much better. One reason I use so many perennials and grasses as opposed to shrubs, is because of their ability to rejuvenate following cutting back; making them exceptionally useful in areas prone to accidental damage or vandalism. The fresh growth of grasses and herbaceous perennials in spring makes an appreciable difference to plantings - announcing a new season.

Deciduous grasses are best cut back before the spring growth begins; I usually do the cutting back in late winter, when the wind and rain have started to weaken and reduce last year's foliage. As soon as the grasses look untidy and loose foliage is blowing all around the garden, their task of providing winter interest is finished, and it's time to cut back.

The grasses can be cut quite close to the ground if growth has not yet begun, and this will allow maximum light onto fresh new shoots as they emerge in spring. If necessary, the cutting may be done a little higher to avoid damaging nearby bulb leaves, or if the grasses are already growing strongly from the base. If some of the new growth is inevitably trimmed during the cutting back, it really doesn't matter; the grasses grow strongly in response to increased daylight, and spring temperatures.

The best way of cutting back large grasses is to tie them around the middle using a bungee cord, and cut through close to the ground using a cordless hedge trimmer. The sheaf usually falls away to the side, or might need pushing away from the cutting blades as the tool works through the dead stems; and the whole bundle can easily be picked up and bagged for recycling. Smaller bungee cords come in useful when changing seasonal plants in planters, which have a central grass as a focal point. The cord keeps the grass foliage temporarily tied up, so the annuals can be replaced; the accessible growing medium may be changed at the same time, and slow release fertilizer added.

I don't tend to have many seasonal planters, and never any hanging baskets; where planters are used, they serve a specific purpose, and always have grasses in to minimise discarding annuals. As the central grasses grow, some planters cease to require the addition of annuals, and make a simple, elegant feature in areas such as patios, which cannot otherwise be planted. Planters can also serve as traffic management devices in shared spaces - I use half wine barrels to prevent inappropriate parking and damage to paving slabs, especially by delivery vehicles. These are not easily damaged or moved, especially with approximately 25kg of gravel in the bottom to aid drainage.

Sometimes, a plant may need to be moved to a more suitable location, or to balance the planting with a subtle tweak to the design. If the planting is already quite mature, this kind of adjustment should be unnoticeable to maintain continuity. It's better to put larger plants into an established planting, otherwise a young plant may struggle to find room to extend its roots and thrive. I use bamboo canes to hold back the foliage of nearby plants, so there is room to work.

Finally, the mechanical tools that I use every day are all powered by rechargeable batteries (which are safer than corded mains supply), and more pleasant to use than the petrol equivalents. Noise is kept to a minimum; there are no fumes, and no flammable liquid to transport around and mix with oil. The production and marketing of any tool will cause some pollution; but provided the electricity to recharge the batteries is supplied from a renewable source, there are clear benefits for the immediate and wider environment when using cordless technology.

The maintenance of our shared spaces makes a statement - it says that we care about our environment and our well-being. The positive affect of having planted spaces around us is well documented, and as gardeners we have a collective responsibility not only to maintain, but to improve our surroundings. Our work shapes opinions, provokes comments and emotional responses - people really do care about the views they see every day.

The photograph above, and front cover/introduction pictures were taken at Woolley, Beardsleys & Bosworth LLP, Loughborough during 2019. I have used similar pictures to show seasonal alteration, and the way in which grasses and perennials catch the sunlight, making the same view appear different as the day progresses. All the photographs in this book were taken using a Panasonic DMC-FZ200 digital camera.

Lexicon

Annuals - plants with a life cycle that lasts only one year.

Bedding - the temporary, seasonal use of mainly annual plants to create colourful displays.

Climatic - relating to climate/general weather conditions.

Crown - the parts of a plant growing above ground.

Culm - stem of grass or bamboo.

Deadheading - remove dead flower heads from a plant.

Deciduous - a plant that sheds its leaves annually.

Division - to separate a growing plant which has multiple stems into smaller pieces.

Ecological - the relationship of living organisms to one another and to their physical surroundings.

Ecosystem - a biological community of interacting organisms and their physical environment.

Eurasian - from Europe and Asia.

Exotic - a term used to describe non-native plants.

Flocculate - fine soil particles join together into larger structures called aggregates.

Frost heave - plants and soil are lifted up when ice forms in the soil during freezing conditions.

Genera - plural of genus.

Genus - a group of plants or animals with similar characteristics, usually containing several species.

Groundcover - plants used as mulch to cover the ground under or around larger plants.

Habitat - the environment in which a plant normally lives; the place where something is commonly found.

Hardiness - the ability of a plant to survive outside during winter.

Hardy perennial - a plant that lives for more than 2 years and is capable of surviving low winter temperatures.

Herbaceous perennial - a plant that lives for more than 2 years, and has no woody (lignified) stems. The foliage usually dies back completely in winter, regenerating in spring.

Hybrid - a plant arising from the cross-breeding of dissimilar plants, either naturally or artificially.

Medium - compost mixture or other material in which plants are grown in containers. Growing mediums are collectively called media.

Microclimate - the climate of a very small or restricted area, especially when this differs from the climate of the surrounding area.

Monoculture - growth consisting of a single plant type in a given area.

Mulch - material such as decaying leaves, woodchips or compost, spread around plants or used to cover areas of bare topsoil. Living mulch consists of groundcover plants.

Nativar - a variety of plant selected from a native species, and marketed as a cultivar. It may occur naturally, or by selective breeding.

Native - plants considered indigenous (naturally occurring) in a region, or habitat without human introduction.

Naturalistic - resembling something that exists in nature.

Pathogen - an organism that causes disease.

Perennial - a plant that lives for more than 2 years; in horticulture the term excludes trees, shrubs and bulbs. In this book, the term perennial is used to describe plants that have no woody (lignified) stems, and includes both evergreen and herbaceous perennials.

Pollinator - an insect or other agent that transfers pollen. This transfer may be within the same flower; between different flowers on the same plant; or flowers on another plant of the same species.

Rhizome - a type of plant stem, under or touching the soil surface, capable of producing roots, stems, leaves and flowers.

Self-sustaining - able to continue in a healthy state without outside assistance.

Species - a group of plants or animals within a genus, with the ability to reproduce.

Stolon - an above ground plant stem, producing new plants.

Subshrub - a perennial plant having a woody (lignified) base and partially soft stems, or a small shrub.

Systemic - affecting the whole of something.

Temperate - a region or climate with generally mild temperatures.

Thinning - to reduce in number by removing some plants.

Underplant - to plant smaller plants around a larger plant.

Printed in Great Britain
by Amazon